grief

grief

A Biblical Pathway to God

BISHOP JOEY JOHNSON

*Foreword by Russell Friedman
of The Grief Recovery Institute*

Grief: A Biblical Pathway to God
by Bishop Joey Johnson

Cover Design by Atinad Designs.

© Copyright 2016

SAINT PAUL PRESS, DALLAS, TEXAS

First Printing, 2016

ISBN-10: 1533603596
ISBN-13: 978-1533603593

Printed in the U.S.A.

contents

foreword

I am writing this foreword on Saturday, November 14th, 2015, the day after the horrific attacks in Paris. My heart, like the hearts of most people I know, is heavy with grief on behalf of the people directly and indirectly affected by the attacks. It is also weighed down with my own fears and doubts as this attack has one more time reminded us all of the fragility and transience of this thing called life.

I don't have a solution to the world's problems any more than the next fellow, but I do believe that the friendship Bishop Joey and I have carved out, from often diametrically opposed positions, could be a template for peace, connection, and harmony.

It all started in 2002, when an exceptional dialogue began between me and then Pastor, now Bishop, Joey Johnson. Respectful titles notwithstanding, I tend to think of him as my friend, my brother, Joey. I can't tell you how many late nights I spent typing up responses to the questions, challenges, and debates contained in the emails Joey sent me. Nor can I tell you how many times my wife would say, "Are you coming to bed, honey?" I would reply, "In a minute." And that minute would stretch into hours.

Truth be told—and truth must always and only be told—Joey and I were 180% apart on several issues. As I think about it some 13 years later, I realize those late night back and forth were each of our attempts to change the other person and bring him around to our point-of-view. I'm sure I don't have to tell you that never happened.

But what I do want to tell you is about the elegance and grace with which it did not happen. I want to tell you about the bond that was created then, and has been cemented over time, and especially recently as we worked together to iron out some elements of this book so they truly represent both our points-of-view in a way that will be of immense value for you.

As Joey and I exchanged those emails back in the day, each of us expressing tremendous passion and conviction about what we believed, there was never an *ad hominem* personal attack, never a lack of respect, and never an absence of dignity, given and received. The tone and attitude were always of the highest order, which I believe allowed each of us to be as honest and forthright as possible in expressing what we each believed to be the "truth."

If I had a magic wand, the first thing I would do would be to wave it over every human being and invest in them the ability to listen to and talk with others the way we did, and still do.

Some of the Whys and Why Nots of Grief Recovery

As Bishop Joey points out throughout this book, The Grief Recovery Method® is neither anti-religious nor anti-spiritual, but many people incorrectly think it is because it apparently doesn't use direct religious principles as the foundation of the actions of grief recovery.

However, if you were to attend one of our lectures, workshops, or trainings, you would hear several references directly from the bible. The most obvious—something everyone knows—is the shortest scripture in the English language version of the Christian bible, "Jesus wept." We use it to counteract the illogically tragic idea that most of us learn in childhood, which is to not feel bad or sad, when something bad or sad has affected our hearts.

We intone it because grievers' sadness is often met with well-meaning but incorrect ideas like, "Don't feel bad, he/she is in a better place," or "Don't feel bad, God won't give you more than you can handle." [That last, usually said to someone who is drowning in sorrow.] We ask, if Jesus wept when his friend Lazarus died, then why are we told not to feel bad? Makes no sense. Another counter-point to the constant barrage grievers hear, telling them not to feel bad or sad, comes from Proverbs 25:20, which we paraphrase in modern language to say: "Singing cheerful songs to a heavy heart, is as bad as stealing someone's cloak in the winter or pouring salt on their wounds." The obvious point, not dissimilar to "Jesus wept," is that it is normal and natural to feel sad in response to a sad event, and that any attempt to rob someone of those feelings is a grievous error. In order to make the point even more strongly we ask this: "If you tell me you've had a really great day, and everything is going well in your life, would I tell you, 'Don't feel good!'?" Sounds silly, or worse, doesn't it?

We don't do anyone a favor when we attempt to rob them of their feelings, either sad or happy.

To Scripture or Not to Scripture – that is the Riddle

Lastly, I want to use a scriptural passage to explain why we don't use scripture within the books or programs of the Grief Recovery Method®. I know that sounds like a riddle but here you go:

In theory—though not always not in reality—we are each allotted a normal life span that in today's world tends to average 71.0 overall, divided into 68.5 years for men, and 73.5 years for women. That is not to say that we are not heavily saddened when our spouse or one of our relatives or friends who has reached those ages, dies. But the fact that they lived to that average, makes it somewhat easier for us to accept the death, and not feel robbed the way we often do when a child dies, or, in fact, when someone important to us dies who hasn't reached or come close to those average ages.

Add to that, the sometimes horrific way deaths happen that cause us to question everything we believe and believe in, including God. When you've had as many phone calls and personal interactions as I've had with people who had their two year-old child run over and killed by a drunk driver [sorry for the graphic image], then you begin to realize the level and degree to which an untimely and/or horrible death and can breach someone's faith in God.

For many God-loving people, it is almost impossible to reconcile the loving God they believe in and trust, with the kind of tragedy that took their child's life. [That is not limited to the death of a child.] Without going into great detail here, suffice it to say that certain kinds of grief events carry with them the high probability of creating an instant breach of faith in God.

We know this because so many of our Grief Recovery Method® groups are conducted in churches. We also know that devastated grievers, struggling with a major breach from God, may show up at our programs. If they are then asked to pray to the God they feel in conflict with, they will either leave the group—and often the church altogether—or they will stay and lie. Since the principles and actions of the Grief Recovery Method® program are predicated on telling the truth, that griever, for all intents and purposes is lost.

Now let's apply some scripture:

The parable of the lost sheep—Luke 15:4—asks: "What man of you, having a hundred sheep, if he has lost one of them, does not leave the ninety-nine in the open country, and go after the one that is lost, until he finds it?"

The answer is you do leave the ninety-nine out in the open to go find the lost one. We re-state that to say, "If one of our flock is lost, then we are all lost."

That is why our Grief Recovery Method® programs, though mostly presented in churches, do not start with or include prayers. We don't want to risk that the one griever in the group, who may be afraid to say she/he is having a breach of faith, will lose the benefit of the Grief Recovery Method®.

Why do we feel so strongly about it? Over the 37 years that the Grief Recovery Method® program has been functioning in churches, and other venues, we've discovered that when we are able to help the grieving mother, father, and other family members become emotionally complete with the child who died [or any other loss], their faith in the Lord tends to return naturally. If not, we have been able to adapt the principles and actions of our program to help them become emotionally complete with God, or God's local representative [the clergy], or sometimes the tenets of the church that trouble them.

A Few Words About Bishop Joey

My first few words are a question: Can we clone Bishop Joey? Why? Because our stated mission is "to help the largest amount of grieving people in the shortest time possible." And honestly, as I sit here today, I don't know of any other individual who has done as much as he has to help us deliver on that promise.

In addition to taking as many as a thousand people

[or more] through our program, he has encouraged and sponsored scores of others to become Certified Grief Recovery Specialists®. They in turn, have taken thousands more through the program.

John and I are grateful, beyond words, to have Bishop Joey be such an important part of our lives and our mission. Since words really don't do justice, I'll end this note with a giant hug from us to you and to all your congregants and friends.

Brother, Russell Friedman
And for John W. James
November, 14, 2015 - Sherman Oaks, California

Grief: A Biblical Pathway To God

Getting Our Hearts Back

I have been a certified Grief Recovery Specialist since July of 2002. And *The Grief Recovery Method*® has changed my life. Prior to certification, I was fascinated with grief and I had read many books on the subject. During 2001, a gentleman from my church named Art Lee came up to me and said, "I think you might be interested in this book" and handed me *The Grief Recovery Handbook*®. The rest is history!

I began to scour the book and I was fascinated with what I was learning.

No one told me that I couldn't do the exercises that were explained, so I began doing them and the transformation began.

Later, Art Lee came back to me and told me that he was doing grief work with a local hospital in Akron, Ohio and that it was possible to be certified.

Since I had already read the book, done the

exercises, started teaching and preaching on it at church, I took most of my senior staff to a certification. I knew that grief would be a major area of ministry for our staff and our church.

One of our staff members, Pastor Pam Ecrement—who oversaw Grief Ministry for over ten years, is a marriage and family therapist. She attended certification with us.

I believe it was after the certification process that I looked at Pastor Pam and said, "I don't want to be working on grief recovery for the next 30 years, so how would you like to do some major work together?" She enthusiastically agreed! So, when we returned from the certification, we met every Thursday for about three months and worked on three people on our Loss History Graphs in each meeting.

I did The Grief Recovery Method® work on over 30 people and I continued to do the work on any new losses to the present time. If doing work on one person is getting out of solitary confinement, then doing work on every person on your Loss History Graph is getting out of prison!

Pastor Pam is the only other person, that I know personally, who has done as much work as I have.

Since that time, I have conducted many Grief Recovery Groups, Reunion Groups, Helping Children Grieve Groups, and Introductory Workshops, preached on the subject and taken many people through the method one-on-one.

During the early days of my work with The Grief

Recovery Method®, I was struggling with how to do the method in a church context. The Grief Recovery Method® is an educational program, not an intellectual program or spiritual program. Yet, Christianity is a core belief that I could not get away from. In fact, we say, "Sometimes, God just won't stay out of Grief Recovery!"

So, I began to talk to Russell Friedman about how to deal with God in conjunction with The Grief Recovery Method®. Russell warned me concerning the complications and helped me create a disclaimer to use at the beginning of our groups.

Disclaimer

Grief Recovery is an educational program, the actions of which may help the human spirit soar. Many people whose faith has been damaged by an overwhelming loss, or by an accumulation of losses, over a lifetime, have discovered that these actions free their spirit and actually enhance their relationship with God, and with their spiritual principles.

Therefore, for this class, we will usually not pray, either at the beginning or at the end. We believe that when we lead, influence, or force people to pray to God, when they have a breach in their relationship with God, we impact their emotional honesty and make it difficult for them to resolve their relationships with other people and God.

The goal of Grief Recovery is to help people recover from loss or complete loss events and get their hearts back. We do not want to put people in conflict with their desire to tell the truth. Once they get their hearts back, they can move forward and resolve or complete pain in all of their relationships, including their relationship with God.

Let me be clear: I'm not suggesting that you mix spirituality, theology, and the Bible into The Grief Recovery Method®. I have found that some church people will try to spiritualize the method, rather than work through the process.

However, I often conduct The Grief Recovery Method® in churches and some churches, reformations, and church people have a great deal of difficulty going through a program that they view as extra-biblical or anti-biblical.

Therefore, I developed a biblical perspective of The Grief Recovery Method® for those who need to validate or defend their usage of this tool; and for those who just want to know how it correlates with the Bible.

chapter one

An Introduction to Grief Recovery®

Grief is a spiritual discipline of the Christian life that seems to be neglected by much of the Christian world. But, before I can talk about that, I need to tell you a little bit of my story as a backdrop to the aforementioned evaluation.

I have been reading and personally studying the field of grief, since Elizabeth Kubler-Ross first began to deal with the experiences of those who were dying. Her studies and observations originally had to do with the experiences of those who were dying, but there was also some speculation about their families and what they were experiencing. Later, she and others began to recognize that the families of dying people were also grieving. And still later, it was recognized that grief extended beyond the loss of death to other losses.

Well, I began to read everything that I could get my hands on concerning grief. I began to see that everybody has pain and losses that they are grieving. Their grieving may be healthy or unhealthy; freeing or imprisoning; pain perpetuating or pain completing.

For twenty years I continued to read on the subject, because the reading was generally good, but none of it seemed to include any specific steps or how-to's with respect to working through or recovering from grief.

In 2001, after Art Lee handed me the book and said something to the effect of, "I think you might be interested in this book. It contains some how-to's with respect to grief and I have been doing some grief groups." I was exposed to a tool that I did not know existed!

I read the book and found it fascinating—just as he had suggested. The book had some great information in it, but it also had some how-to's with respect to recovering from grief.

I believe in the effectiveness of The Grief Recovery Method® and highly recommended it.

Yet, I ran into a problem! As a pastor of a Christian Church that has strong roots in the Bible, it seemed incongruent to me to use something that didn't talk about God.

I talked with Russell Friedman about this and he was wonderful. He explained to me that Grief Recovery® is not an intellectual, religious, or biblical program, but an educational program the actions of which have helped people complete their relationship to certain pain.

Russell gave me a lot of warnings, and I took each one of them very seriously.

After carefully listening to Russell, I realized that I had done some things that I probably shouldn't have done and would not recommend to anyone else, but I was still facing a major obstacle: "How do I work with people whose values and lives revolve around God and the Bible and completely ignore how The Grief Recovery Method® integrates with those values and the Bible?"

After much thought and prayer, I decided that I could not—in good conscience—ignore God and the Bible and just do The Grief Recovery® Program.

Furthermore, having been a pastor for more than 30 years, I knew that many Pastors who respect the Word of God and use it as their grid for all truth, would not be open to a program that avoided the Bible. Whether the program was anti-biblical or extra-biblical, it still needed to be filtered through the sieve of the Word of God.

Knowing that the Grief Recovery Method® was not anti-biblical, I felt impressed to correlate the two— not only for those in my church, but for those who need a biblical base to assure that they are not violating their own biblical integrity by using the program.

On Monday afternoon, November 18th, 2002, I had another epiphany. They seemed to come more rapidly and more powerfully, perhaps because of the grief work that I had done...perhaps because I was fifty years old at the time...perhaps because of all the reading I had done...perhaps because of the years of struggling and surrendering my life to God, through ministry...perhaps?

As I was coming to the end of reading *The Journey of Desire*, by John Eldredge, I came across this paragraph, "I believe we must add two spiritual disciplines to everyday life. The first is worship. We must adore God deliberately, regularly. The other is grief. We must allow a time of sorrow to do our own personal sowing. I see no other way to care for our hearts."[1]

After reading this, the following truth broke upon me like the newborn sun breaking over the horizon and into my room on an expectant spring morning: The Grief Recovery Method® is but a tool, a very excellent tool, but alas...still a tool. There is a spiritual discipline associated with *grieving* that is put forth and described in the Bible; experienced by Jesus Christ to procure our salvation and to be our example; and arranged by the Father to cleanse and heal our hearts and woo us back to Himself, where He will one day wipe away every loss, pain, sorrow, sadness, and grief in heaven.

Until then, we must allow time for suffering, sorrow, and grief to do their perfect work. Is that what the psalmist realized in Psalm 126:4-6 (NLT), "Restore our fortunes, LORD, as streams renew desert? Those who plant in tears will harvest with shouts of joy. They weep as they go to plant their seed, but they sing as

---

[1] John Eldredge, *The Journey Of Desire*, Thomas Nelson Publishers, Nashville, Tennessee, 2000, p. 189.

they return with the harvest."

Sorrow is our sowing and rejoicing is our reaping! As we continue to make time for personal times of sowing, we shall reap more and more joy. It is grief that will circumcise and prepare our hearts for true, living, intimate worship of Jehovah God. It is grief that will allow us to be fully present enough to give all that we are in worship to God, because of all that He is. It is grief that will allow us to enter into passionate, unabashed, delicious, breathtaking intimacy with the Lover of our Souls, i.e. Jesus Christ!

As "praise is a means of taking territory back from the devil" and "worship is the means of ratifying the covenant promises of God," so grief is the means of recapturing and living through our hearts, so that praise and worship might be released unto their full potential.

We are most alive when we are genuinely worshipping God, and grief keeps the lifeblood of worship flowing.

So, I did a six-message series on The Grief Recovery® Program where I set a biblical basis for the program.

Disclaimer

I believe in the effectiveness of The Grief Recovery® Program as it is. I am not suggesting that it be done any other way than the way one is taught to do it in certification. I am not suggesting that those who are certified begin to integrate my biblical beliefs *into their groups. In fact, I suggest that you don't do that. I have chosen to do this, because I have read extensively on grief, done a great deal of group facilitation, and have thought and prayed deeply on the relationship between grief and the Bible.*

Therefore, I am writing this book to assure those who want to use The Grief Recovery Method® that not only is it not anti-biblical, but that the actions highly correspond to biblical actions. This will allow you to feel comfortable that you are not violating your own biblical integrity by using The Grief Recovery Method®.

**The Impediment To Intimacy
(How To Get Our Hearts Back)**

chapter two

The Heart of the Matter 1

I believe the major impediment to intimacy with God is disappointment with God that flows from unresolved or incomplete grief issues. And again, as normal, God is using me to highlight and teach on a subject that is rarely touched on. *God has called me to provoke deep Biblical consideration of biblical realities that people habitually prefer not to consider, for the purpose of facilitating encounters with God, Jesus, the Christ, and the Holy Spirit.* Consequently, the most off-limits topic of conversation in the United States is grief. We don't have any problem talking about dying, death, sex, etc., but we shrink back from discussing grief.

It is my ministerial and personal thrust to help believers come into deep intimacy with God through the baptism in and/or control by the Holy Ghost. The ministry of the Holy Spirit is connected to intimacy with God. *But, unresolved grief, with the specific fruit of disappointment in God, seems to be blocking American believers from deeply experiencing and enjoying intimacy with God.*

Please note that disappointment in God may be conscious or unconscious.

Keep in mind that there are many potential loss experiences that one can have in his/her lifetime. The Grief Recovery Method® defines grief as "the conflicting feelings that come at the change in any normal pattern of behavior."[2]

These experiences include the death of a loved one, the death of a less than loved one, divorce, moving, loss of a job, etc., etc., etc. This list also includes changes in normal patterns of behavior, like obtaining a loan, which also impact similarly to loss events.

In fact, life can be looked at as a series of <u>losses</u>:
- when we are born, we lose the warm, secure environment of the womb;
- as we grow we lose our innocence;
- when we go to school, we must lose some of our dependence upon mom;
- when we get to school and pass to the next grade,

---

2 John W. James and Russell Friedman, The Grief Recovery Handbook, HarperCollins Publishers. Inc., New York, New York, 1998, p. 3.

- we lose some of our acquaintances and friends;
- we get toys and teeth that we eventually lose;
- we lose pets;
- as we grow older we lose fitness, stamina, looks, etc.; and
- we lose loved ones.

The authors of *The Grief Recovery Handbook*® state, "After twenty years of working with grievers, we have identified several other losses, including loss of trust, loss of safety, and loss of control of one's body (physical or sexual abuse). (*Even though*) **Society still does not recognize these losses as grief issues.**"[3]

It is also important that we understand something about loss-of-trust events, because they are so prevalent in American society and culture. Loss-of-trust events are experienced by everyone and *they are blocking our intimacy with God.*

Before we go any further, we need to go back to the beginning of Humanity to understand my contention that the major impediment to intimacy with God is disappointment with God, which flows from unresolved or incomplete loss issues.

In the beginning, according to the book of beginnings, i.e. the Bible-book of Genesis, we were created for perfect intimacy in the Garden of Eden. In the sermon series, "The Importance of Intimacy," I took the time to define and describe intimacy. In that series, I defined

---

3 John W. James and Russell Friedman, The Grief Recovery Handbook, HarperCollins Publishers. Inc., New York, New York, 1998, p. 5.

"intimacy" as two hearts shaking hands.

In this God-created beginning of Humanity, Adam and Eve were innocent. **There were no loss events, because there was no sin.** Our hearts were innocent and unencumbered by sin or losses. There had never been a loss for Humanity, and then suddenly it happened! Satan, tempted Adam and Eve and they fell from their innocence through sin and rebellion against God.

With this event, everything changed! With the Fall of Adam and Eve and the entrance of sin into the stream of Humanity, there came into being loss events and something happened to our hearts. **Sin is a loss event in and of itself and sin precipitates all other loss events.** Let me say that again, "All loss events flow from the very first lost event."

We want to talk about what the first loss event and subsequent loss events do to our hearts, but we cannot do that without first establishing the importance of the heart and what we mean when we use the term "heart."

So, let's take the time to talk about the concept of the heart, especially because of its contrast with the concept of the head.

First of all the Bible is a book mostly concerned with the heart, <u>not</u> the head. I know that sounds strange and like blasphemy to some of you, but just hang with me. *The Bible is a Hebrew book, written mostly by Hebrews, in the context of Hebrew society and culture.* Even though New Testament was written in *Koine* Greek, which is the common language of the people during the time of Christ, it was written with a decidedly Hebrew flavor. In addition, the Israelites were much more concerned with concepts like the heart, soul, spirit, etc., while the Greeks were much more concerned with concepts like the mind, intellect, thoughts, etc.

In contrast, it is not the Hebrew mindset, but the Greek mindset that has heavily influenced America, and the impact of the Enlightenment and Greek thinking upon American thought and theology has caused an elevating of thoughts over feelings.

Furthermore, I believe a territorial spirit called the prince of Greece, in Daniel 10:20, has a great deal of influence in America. *In America, a tremendous amount of teaching goes on that seems to suggest that you apprehend or understand spiritual truth through the mind or intellect, while the Bible is clear that the human spirit is the faculty for apprehending spiritual truth, and the human spirit is often used interchangeably with the heart or is seen as the heart of the heart.* This may seem strange, because most of the preaching that is done in America is done through the Greek mindset and is filtered through the theological propositions of the Apostle Paul.

But, if Paul were listened to more closely, in the original culture and context in which he wrote, we might be able to see our error. For instance, it was Paul who wrote in 1 Corinthians 1:22-24 (NASB-U),

> "For indeed Jews ask for signs and **Greeks search for wisdom**; but we preach Christ crucified, to Jews a stumbling block and to Gentiles foolishness, but to those who are the called, both Jews and Greeks, Christ the power of God and the wisdom of God" (*bold type added*).

It was Paul who also wrote:

> 1 Corinthians 2:1-5 (NASB-U), "And when I came to you, brethren, I did not come with superiority of speech or of wisdom, proclaiming to you the testimony of God. For I determined to know nothing among you except Jesus Christ, and Him crucified. I was with you in weakness and in fear and in much trembling, and my message and my preaching were not in persuasive words of wisdom, but in demonstration of the Spirit and of power, so that your faith would not rest on the wisdom of men, but on the power of God."

> 1 Corinthians 2:14 (NASB-U), "But a natural man does not accept the things of the Spirit of

God, for they are foolishness to him; and he cannot understand them, because they are spiritually appraised."

Paul was a Hebrew whose Hebrew culture impacted all that he was and all that he wrote. He wrote in Philippians 3:2-6 (NASB),

"Beware of the dogs, beware of the evil workers, beware of the false circumcision; for we are the *true* circumcision, who worship in the Spirit of God and glory in Christ Jesus and put no confidence in the flesh, although I myself might have confidence even in the flesh. If anyone else has a mind to put confidence in the flesh, I far more: circumcised the eighth day, of the nation of Israel, of the tribe of Benjamin, a Hebrew of Hebrews; as to the Law, a Pharisee; as to zeal, a persecutor of the church; as to the righteousness which is in the Law, found blameless."

Spiritual truth is <u>not</u> apprehended through the rational processes of the gray matter of the brain, but through receiving spiritual revelation in our human spirits and hearts from the Spirit of Truth, the Holy Spirit. This is not to say that our brains are not important in processing spiritual truth or not needed at all, but rather that they are not the primary faculty for apprehending spiritual truth, encountering God, or communing with God. *God is not a brain, God is a Persons, i.e. one God in three persons, personas or personalities! God doesn't even have a brain. God is spirit and God has intuition!* Intuition is the ability to know information without the conscious use of reason. God simply knows all things! Yet, God's personality is more than intuition. If we liken God's personality to our human personalities, since we are made in the image of God, as we have intellect, emotion, and will God has intuition, communion, and conscience. Just as God is more than intuition and has a heart, we, are more than intellects and have hearts!

So, what's the problem? *The problem lies in the fact that I believe most Americans are subconsciously intimidated by intimacy.* We have been so impacted by the Enlightenment, Rationalism, Modernism and the Greek-oriented mode of thinking, that we have seriously minimized the emotional and spiritual aspects of Humanity. We have so minimized them that we have become uncomfortable with them and intimidated by them. So, we must begin to understand the human heart from a biblical perspective.

You are probably wondering what my evidence is for my perspective of the heart.

- My perspective comes from reading and studying the Bible since I was eight years old, and I am now sixty-three.
- My perspective comes from reading through the Bible more than 40 times in many different

translations.

- My perspective comes from the ongoing study and reading that I do for devotion and sermon preparation.

The word "heart" comes up 725 times, in the O.T. of the KJV.

The word "heart" comes up 105 times, in the N.T. of the KJV.

The words "mind" and "will" come up far, far fewer times.

In addition, I have reviewed every occurrence of the word "heart" and all of the Hebrew and Greek words that are translated "heart," in the Bible. This is neither the time nor place for this information—not to mention the fact that it would be incredibly boring to most of you reading this book. Nevertheless, it is extremely important. Therefore, allow me to use a summary of the meaning of the word "heart," from Colin Brown's *The New International Dictionary of New Testament Theology.* This source says, "However, in its abstract meanings, 'heart' became the richest biblical term for the totality of man's inner or immaterial nature. In biblical literature it is the most frequently used term for man's immaterial personality functions as well as the most inclusive term for them since, in the Bible, virtually every immaterial function of man is attributed to the 'heart.'"

In short, the general use of the term "heart," in the Bible is the totality of the intellect, emotion, and will.

The heart is the whole personality of a person and there can be no genuine encounter with God except through the heart or the human spirit, which is the heart of the heart, and the heart of the heart requires the whole heart.

If you know anything about the Tabernacle of Moses, the structure can be used as a metaphor of a saved Human Being.

I'm using the concepts of intellect, emotion and will because we are so familiar with them. The Bible uses the concepts of body, soul, and spirit.

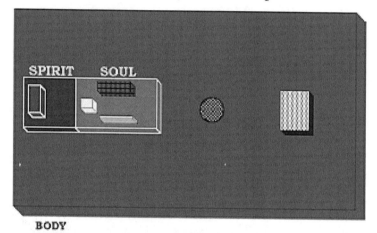

The Tabernacle Floor Plan

- The wall of curtains (or outer border) represents human skin.
- The outer court represents the body or material part of Humanity.
- The Tabernacle building represents the soul/ spirit or the immaterial part of Humanity.
- The first room is the Holy Place and it represents

the heart or soul of Humanity, with three pieces of furniture: the light of the Golden Lampstand which impacts our emotions; the Table of Shewbread which impacts our intellect; and the Golden Altar of Incense or Prayer which interacts with our will.

- The second room is the Holy of Holies and it represents the innermost being or the spirit of a saved Human being.

Please hear me, "I am not suggesting that we ignore or violate our intellect. I am suggesting that there are Human faculties that are just as important as the intellect and in some cases transcend the intellect. One of those faculties is our emotions.

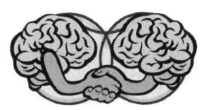

They are an important part of our Humanity, and I am suggesting that we no longer deny our emotions, but begin to understand how those emotions interact with our thoughts to combine in the choices we make and the relationships that we experience.

Some of you are saying so what?

All of this has to do with relationships! We cannot experience the intimacy that God created us to experience, which is the highest level of intimacy, through the exclusive use of our thoughts. In many cases, our relationships are only two brains shaking hands, instead of two hearts shaking hands.

I have a BHAG, which is the acronym for "Big Hairy Audacious Goal." The concept comes from a book entitled, *Built To Last*, by James C. Collins and Jerry I. Porras, HarperBusiness, HarperCollins Publishers, New York, New York, 1994. The book is a six-year research project that compares visionary companies with a carefully selected controlled set of comparison companies. A BHAG is not a purpose statement, not a vision statement, not a motto, not a plan, but a goal or miracle that will take supernatural intervention.

My BHAG is to change the world's concept of Christianity from reason-centered to relationship-centered. The diagram depicts, on the left, two brains shaking hands or agreeing on the propositions of the Bible, while, on the right, we have two hearts agreeing on the truths of the Bible as revealed through the living ministry of the Holy Spirit.

In the visual representation of my BHAG, I am working to facilitate a movement from two brains shaking hands under the rational truth of the Bible to two hearts shaking hands through the power of the Holy Spirit in keeping with the revealed truth of the Bible.

- Christianity is **not** a doctrine.
- Christianity is **not** a set of theological propositions.
- Christianity is **not** an intellectual knowledge.
- Christianity is **not** a set of rules.

Christianity is a relationship with Jesus Christ!

Now some of you should be thinking, "Why do we need to get our hearts back?"

The answer to that question is critical. I will answer that in detail in the coming chapters. Right now let me give you an introductory answer. **We need to get our hearts back, because sin causes a hardness of the heart!** Each loss that is not completed or resolved develops a little area of hardness or protection around it so that it doesn't hurt again. In effect, that part of our heart becomes unavailable to anyone in the future, including God.

Once again, you may be thinking, "So what?"

Well, let's consider a very powerful word from God in Jeremiah 29:13 (NASB-U), "You will seek Me and find Me when you search for Me with all your heart."

Although this was written to the ancient Hebrews, it is very applicable to us today. To find God, we must seek Him with all of our heart, i.e. our intellect, emotions, and choices or our bio-psycho-spiritual being. This is where the trouble starts. We cannot bring the emotions of our hearts to God, because they are walled off. Therefore, we cannot bring all of our hearts to God. Pieces of our hearts have been lost in each unresolved grief event. This causes us to be closed and separated, as opposed to open and connected. God did not create us to be closed and separated, but open and connected, i.e. intimate—with Him and with one another.

So, what's the answer?

In this introductory chapter, I only give a preliminary answer that I will develop throughout the book. The answer is **deep repentance**, which I believe often needs a tool like The Grief Recovery Method®.

For right now, let me ask you, "Do you have the same sentiments as David?" In repenting for his adulterous and murderous acts in connection with Bathsheba, David wrote in Psalm 51:10 (NASB-U), "Create in me a clean heart, O God, and renew a steadfast spirit within me."

This is what we are talking about! We need a clean heart or we need to regain the hardened pieces of our hearts, and whatever happens in the heart deeply affects the human spirit—the heart of the heart!

Would you join me in seeking God for a clean heart, a new heart, a whole heart?

chapter three

The Heart of the Matter 2

The psalmist sings of an event that involves hardness of heart in Psalm 95:8 (NASB-U), "Do not harden your hearts, as at Meribah, as in the day of Massah in the wilderness."

Do you know that story? Well, the Bible says in Exodus 17:1-7 that when the Children of Israel were traveling through the wilderness, and there was no water to drink, the people quarreled with Moses and said, "Give us water to drink." Moses said to the people, "Why are you quarreling with me? Why do you test the

Lord?" Nevertheless, the people continued to complain against Moses and the Lord said to Moses to stand in front of the people and to strike the rock at Horeb, so that water might come out of it for the people to drink. "And Moses did so in the sight of the elders of Israel. And he named the place Massah and Meribah because of the quarrel of the sons of Israel, and because they tested the Lord, saying, 'Is the Lord among us, or not?'" David asked the Israelites of his day not to harden their hearts, as they did in this situation at Massah and Meribah. Because their hearts were hardened, the Israelites grumbled against Moses, God's leader, and tested the LORD, i.e. God. How did they test God, "They asked the question, "Is the LORD among us?" *They questioned God's presence among them, because He was not giving them what they wanted!*

Disappointment with God was blocking their intimacy with Him.

The Israelites' hardness of heart was an ongoing problem. God said in Numbers 14:22-23 (NASB-U),

> "Surely all the men who have seen My glory and My signs, which I performed in Egypt and in the wilderness, **yet have put Me to the test these ten times and have not listened to My voice,** shall by no means see the land which I swore to their fathers, nor shall any of those who spurned Me see it."

Hardness of heart caused the Israelites to repeatedly

test the LORD and not listen to His voice. I believe the same thing is happening to modern people!

The issue of the hardness of human hearts is also seen in the New Testament.

> Mark 6:52 (NASB-U), "For they had not gained any insight from the incident of the loaves, but their heart was hardened."

Hardness of heart kept the people from understanding the miracles of Jesus!

Hardness of heart was also seen in the issue of divorce. The Bible says in Mark 10:2-5 (NASB-U),

> "Some Pharisees came up to Jesus, testing Him, and began to question Him whether it was lawful for a man to divorce a wife. And He answered and said to them, 'What did Moses command you?' They said, 'Moses permitted a man to write a certificate of divorce and send her away.' But Jesus said to them, **'Because of your hardness of heart** he wrote you this commandment'" (*bold type added*).

Moses only permitted the Israelites to divorce their wives because of their hardness of heart, not because of the will of God.

In addition to these verses, we find more about hardness of heart in Mark 16:14 (NASB-U),

"Afterward He appeared to the eleven themselves as they were reclining at the table; and He reproached them for their unbelief and **hardness of heart**, because they had not believed those who had seen Him after He had risen" (*bold type added*).

Furthermore, hardness of heart kept the eleven remaining disciples of the Lord—Judas had comitted suicide—from believing the report that He had risen!

Paul also touches on the problem of hardness of heart in Romans 2:4-5 (NASB-U),

"Or do you think lightly of the riches of His kindness and tolerance and patience, not knowing that the kindness of God leads you to repentance? But because of your **stubbornness** and unrepentant heart you are storing up wrath for yourself in the day of wrath and revelation of the righteous judgment of God" (*bold type added*).

Some of you are saying, "I don't see the phrase 'hardness of heart' in these verses?" You are right. The phrase is not there directly, but it is indirectly. *In this particular verse of the Bible, the NASB-U version translates the Greek word "sklērotes" as "stubbornness," but the KJV translates the word "hardness."*

It is also interesting that Paul coupled impenitence

or a lack of repentance with hardness. *So, we can extrapolate that "hardness of heart" is closely related to or the same thing as an unrepentant heart!*

I trust that I have established the fact that hardness of heart is a major Bible subject and issue among Human Beings.

So, what is the answer? According to the previous verse, if a hard and unrepentant heart is a problem, the answer must be the opposite: a soft or repentant heart! Yet, I want to take this one step further. I believe the answer is deep repentance!

I believe there is a major difference between **deep** repentance and **shallow** repentance. Deep repentance penetrates the heart; shallow repentance does not. David experienced *deep* repentance over his sin with Bathsheba, while Esau experienced *shallow* repentance with respect to selling his birthright. David's experience of deep repentance is cataloged for us in the 51st Psalm, so we shall use David's experience of *deep* repentance as the basis of our teaching on repentance. **Keep in mind that the Psalms mention virtually every known feeling or emotion of Humanity.**

But before we begin to talk about David's deep repentance, let's touch on Esau's experience of shallow repentance.

Esau's experience of shallow repentance is summed up in Hebrews 12:15-17 (NASB-U),

"See to it that no one comes short of the grace of God; that no root of bitterness springing up causes trouble, and by it many be defiled; that there be no immoral or godless person like Esau, who sold his own birthright for a single meal. For you know that even afterwards, when he desired to inherit the blessing, he was rejected, **for he found no place for repentance**, though he sought for it with tears" (*bold type added*).

Whatever this verse means, I infer that Esau did not approach repentance with all of his heart, even though he sought it with tears. The Bible tells us that godly sorrow brings about deep repentance, and godly sorrow is more than tears. **Godly sorrow must penetrate every facet of the heart!**

Tears can be a sign of godly sorrow, when they flow from a deeply repentant heart. However, tears alone are not necessarily indicative of a deeply repentant heart. Some people cry because they are caught, not because they are genuinely sorry that they have broken the heart of God. I would define deep repentance as "a decision to turn from sin, based on a correct understanding of the Word of God, with the proper corresponding emotions." **In short, a change of heart!**

Let's just touch on the deep repentance of David, as it is related to us, in Psalm 51.

Psalm 51:10 (NASB-U), "Create in me a clean heart, O God, and renew a steadfast spirit within me."

David sought a clean heart and a renewed spirit! We have already talked about the spirit being the heart of the heart, and the heart of the heart cannot be renewed without impacting the whole heart. *So, David sought an experience with God that would clean and renew his heart. This would certainly change a hardened heart to a heart of flesh, or a sensitive heart.*

We shall return to David and Psalm 51 throughout this book, but for now let's move forward.

The Old Testament also refers to this clean heart, renewed spirit, or deep repentance as a circumcised heart. As the foreskin of the male sexual organ is cut away, which allows it to be more potent in planting seed and creating life, so the foreskin of the heart needs to be cut away, so that it can be more potent in planting *spiritual* seed and creating *spiritual* life.

Many of us are unable to enter into deep intimacy with Jehovah God, because our hearts are impotent.

Let's consider some other Old Testament verses that mention circumcision of the heart.

Moses exhorted the Israelites in Deuteronomy 10:16 (NASB-U),

"So circumcise your heart, and stiffen your neck no longer."

God gives similar words through Jeremiah in Jeremiah 4:4 (NASB-U),

"Circumcise yourselves to the LORD and remove the foreskins of your heart, men of Judah and inhabitants of Jerusalem, or else My wrath will go forth like fire and burn with none to quench it, because of the evil of your deeds."

Even though David didn't use the word "circumcise" with respect to the heart, he seems to ask for the same revealing of his heart in Psalm 139:23-24 (NASB-U),

"Search me, O God, and know my heart; try me and know my anxious thoughts; and see if there be any hurtful way in me, and lead me in the everlasting way."

The concept of having a circumcised heart is also talked about in the New Testament in Romans 2:29 (NASB),

"But he is a Jew who is one inwardly; and circumcision is that which is of the heart, by the Spirit, not by the letter; and his praise is not from men, but from God."

Let me make a major observation: Deep repentance will remedy hardness of heart and resolve loss issues, but deep repentance often takes a tool. In keeping with this metaphor of circumcision, the tool needed is a sharp knife or scalpel. Sounds painful doesn't it! That's because it is! Deep repentance or cutting away those things that inhibit the heart is not a light, happy, or pleasurable operation or process.

The tool that I am suggesting, in this book, is The Grief Recovery Method®. When there has been an overwhelming loss or an accumulation of losses, there is a hardening of the heart that makes it difficult for deep repentance to be achieved.

Please do not misunderstand me. I never advocate tools in place of the Holy Spirit, but to be facilitated through the power of the Holy Spirit. We came through that era of our church, where I taught all kinds of information and shared all kinds of tools that people liked better than the Bible and used instead of the Bible and without the power of the Holy Spirit. This is not my focus or goal. *I believe that our primary source of help and power should be the Holy Spirit, but sometimes we need a tool to help us deal with ourselves or put us in a position to receive the work and power of the Holy Spirit. A sharp knife cannot wield itself, it begs for a powerful hand to wield it, and that hand is the hand of God.*

In addition, I am not intending to add to, subtract from, or change the actions of the The Grief Recovery Method® in any way, but I do intend to set a Biblical base for its use.

Do you want what David wanted, i.e. a redeemed, whole, and clean heart?

Before we go any further, let's continue setting the context for the Grief Recovery Method®, in the light of Human hardness of heart.

With the entrance of sin and the Fall of Adam and Eve, there came into being loss events. What losses did Adam and Eve experience?

- The loss of intimacy with God.
- The loss of intimacy with each other.
- The loss of intimacy or consistency with self (i.e. disassociation or a lack of integration of their bodies, souls, and spirits).
- The loss of their home (The Garden of Eden).
- The loss of security.
- The loss of significance.
- The loss of innocence.
- The loss of trust.
- The loss of eternal life (death came into the world).

Now, this situation could have been handled immediately with deep repentance. In fact, this situation should have been handled, but it wasn't because of the sinfulness of sin and human proclivities, propensities, or tendencies. **These issues inhibit us from doing the things that we should do to facilitate deep repentance.**

While we are talking about how Adam and Eve had difficulty processing their losses in The Fall, let's also talk about how God handled His losses in connection with that same loss. Why? Because, since we are made in the image of God, we can gain some clues as to how we should have handled our losses connected with The

Fall.

First, let me point out that God grieved over the losses that He experienced in connection with The Fall. It grieved God that He had made Humanity!

Genesis 6:6 (NASB-U), "And the LORD was sorry that He had made man on the earth, and He was grieved in His heart."

We see here, very early in Genesis, that God Himself was grieved in His heart! Why? **God had hopes, dreams, and expectations, which were disappointed when Adam and Eve fell.** It is difficult for us, who see God as "The Great Intellect In The Sky," to see Him with a heart—much less a heart that can be grieved.

But, not only did God grieve concerning Adam and Eve and The Fall, God did His grief work.

How? **Well, first God made no apologies, because He had done nothing wrong.** He had created the beautiful Garden of Eden for His children and given them the run of the Garden with only one prohibition: "Don't eat from the tree of the knowledge of good and evil."

Yet, at the instigation of Satan, Adam and Eve rebelled and sinned against God, while God had done nothing but love them.

Secondly, God made preparations to forgive Adam and Eve of their sins and He also began the process of forgiving and redeeming Humanity. The Bible says in Genesis 3:21 (NASB-U),

"The LORD God made garments of skin for

Adam and his wife, and clothed them."

We assume that God killed animals for those skins. So, the animals were used as sacrifices to substitute for the sins and lives of Adam and Eve. They are a foreshadow of the Lamb of God, who would come to vicariously die for the sins of Humanity. Adam and Eve were forgiven looking forward to the cross; just as we are saved looking back to the cross.

God also made some significant emotional statements. You can see those statements in Genesis 3:8-20. Please look them up and read them at your convenience.

We also see that Jehovah God is not a sick or codependent God, because He set boundaries on Humanity.

Genesis 3:22-24 (NASB-U), "Then the LORD God said, 'Behold, the man has become like one of Us, knowing good and evil; and now, he might stretch out his hand, and take also from the tree of life, and eat, and live forever— therefore the LORD God sent him out from the garden of Eden, to cultivate the ground from which he was taken. So He drove the man out; and at the east of the garden of Eden He stationed the cherubim and the flaming sword which turned every direction to guard the way to the tree of life."

We also see God's grief in

Psalm 116:15 (NASB-U), "Precious in the sight of the LORD Is the death of His godly ones."

Psalm 116:15 (NLT First Edition), "The LORD'S loved ones are precious to him; it grieves him when they die."

Psalm 116:15 (NLT Second Edition), "The LORD cares deeply when his loved ones die."

Psalm 116 is an individual song of thanksgiving. "It was evidently composed for a recitation at a service or thank offering in the temple courts during one of the great festivals."[4] The Psalmist does not relate what happened to him, but instead testifies about what God had done for him. "From what he has experienced, the poet infers that the saints of Jehovah are under His most especial providence."[5] **Precious in the sight of the LORD is the death of His godly ones or Saints!**

Now, what exactly does that mean? I think it means the following:

- God is saddened, when one of His loved ones die.
- God cries when one of His loved ones dies.

4   Leslie C. Allen, *Word Biblical Commentary, Psalms 101-150*, Word Books, Waco, Texas, 1983, p. 114.

5   C. F. Keil and F. Delitzsch, *Commentary On The Old Testament, Volume V, Third Book Of The Psalter*, William B. Eerdmans Publishing Company, Grand Rapids, Michigan, 1988, p. 219.

- God feels the loss of His loved ones from the world situation.
- God feels the pain of His loved ones not being able to continue on with their loved ones.
- God feels the pain of the deceased loved one's family members.
- God feels the loss of the loved one's extended biological family, friends, and church.
- God feels the pain of the groaning and travail of creation.

God's grief is lived out in His "sitting shiva" with His children.

The Jews have a custom called "sitting shiva." "Sitting shiva" is a seven-day mourning period that begins immediately after the funeral of a loved one. The custom is seen in a verse in Genesis, when Joseph was mourning his father. The Egyptians went up with Joseph to bury his father and they observed seven days of mourning with him.

Perhaps this is the situation with Job, when he lost everything and his three friends show up. It says in Job 2:13 (NASB-U),

"Then they sat down on the ground with him for seven days and seven nights with no one speaking a word to him, for they saw that *his* pain was very great."

Maybe we get a glimpse of this in the New

Testament in Matthew 28:19-20 (NASB),

> "Go therefore and make disciples of all the
> nations, baptizing them in the name of the Father
> and the Son and the Holy Spirit, teaching them
> to observe all that I commanded you; and lo, I
> am with you always, even to the end of the
> age."

The term "always" literally means "all days." Jesus promised to be with us through all kinds of days, i.e. dark days, difficult days, despairing days, depressing days, disorienting days, disconcerting days, etc.

Therefore, God is also "sitting shiva" with us on grieving days!

Because God has handled His losses, i.e. resolved or completed His losses, this allows Him to remain a God of the present. The God that we serve is a God of the here and now. This was a part of His covenant name to Israel. When Moses asked God, "Who should I say has sent me," God said to tell them, "I AM WHO I AM." He didn't say, "I was that I was" or "I will be who I will be," but "I AM WHO I AM." God meets us in the present; not in the past or in the future.

We were created to live in present relationship and fellowship with God, ourselves, others, and Creation. Learn to live in the present moment. God lives in the present moment, because His name is "I AM."

Someone wrote the following poem:

I was regretting the past
And fearing the future.
Suddenly my Lord spoke:
"My name is I AM."

He paused
I waited. He continued.

When you live in the past
With its mistakes and regrets, it is hard.
I am not there.
My name is not I WAS.

When you live in the future
with its problems and and fears,
it is hard, I am not there.
My name is not I WILL BE.

When you live in this moment
It is not hard.
I am here.
My name is "I AM."

In fact, grief is a very Biblical concept, and all the members of the Godhead grieve and do their grief work. Not only does God grieve, but Jesus also grieves.

Jesus was a man of sorrows and acquainted with grief.

Isaiah 53:3 (NASB-U), "He was despised and forsaken of men, A man of sorrows and **acquainted** with grief; And like one from whom men hide their face He was despised, and we did not esteem Him" (*bold type added*).

This is a prophetic passage about the coming "Suffering Servant." The "Suffering Servant" typologically represents Jesus, in His first coming. **Jesus, while here on earth, was acquainted with grief.**

The Hebrew word translated "acquainted" means "to know," not simply to be familiar with. Consider his knowledge of grief:

- He came to His own people and His own people rejected Him.
- His disciples abandoned Him in His greatest hour of need.
- His own Father had to turn His back upon Him, when He was on the cross.

In addition, Jehovah God put Jesus to grief to pay for the sins of the world!

Isaiah 53:10 (NASB-U), "But the LORD was pleased to crush Him, putting Him to **grief**; if He would render Himself as a guilt offering, He will see His offspring, He will prolong His days, and the good pleasure of the LORD will prosper in His hand" (*bold type added*).

God, the Son, grieves and does His grief work!
Not only did God the Father and God the Son grieve, but God the Holy Spirit also grieved and did His grief work. We are told **not** to grieve the Holy Spirit.

> Ephesians 4:30 (NASB-U), "And do not **grieve** the Holy Spirit of God, by whom you were sealed for the day of redemption" (*bold type added*).

This is a very remarkable and important Bible verse. The Holy Spirit of God, the third person of the Triune Godhead, can be and often is grieved by our sin. ***God the Holy Spirit does His grief work!***

It is important to understand that: "God **doesn't** need any tools to do His grief work, because His memory is immediate and complete. He doesn't have to work at recalling things. They are all instantly and perfectly known to him.

God **doesn't** need to apologize to us, because He makes no mistakes and does not sin.

God **does** need to forgive us and He does so.

God **also** needs to make significant emotional statements to us and keeps those current, through His Spirit, His Word, and His People.

God has already written His completion letter. It is called the Bible." And, "God reads and writes this letter upon the hearts of those who meet certain conditions.

- God the Father did His grief work.
- God the Son, Jesus, did His grief work.
- God the Holy Spirit did and continues to do His grief work."

I believe I have referenced enough Bible verses for you to see that grief is something God experiences. Being made in the likeness and image of God, we too must do our grief work or repent deeply—if we want to be healthy.

Finally, Paul addresses a major point about grief in our lives in 1 Thessalonians 4:13 (NASB-U),

"But we do not want you to be uninformed, brethren, about those who are asleep, that you may not **grieve**, as do the rest who have no hope."

Paul said that we do **not** have to grieve **like** the world, when we lose someone to death—but we do grieve! So, again, we need to do The Grief Recovery Method®. There is a time to grieve. The writer of the Ecclesiastes teaches us that there is

"A time to cry and a time to laugh. **A time to grieve** and a time to dance" (*bold type added*, Ecclesiastes 3:4)

chapter four

What is the Grief Recovery Method®?

Understanding that The Grief Recovery Method® will sometimes be conducted in churches with church people, I took the time to set a Biblical context for its use and highlighted some of the spiritual principles that underlie The Grief Recovery actions.

In addition to that context and the spiritual principles that we have already touched on, please be aware of the following:

- The Grief Recovery Method® is **not** a spiritual discipline.
- The Grief Recovery Method® is **not** prayer, fasting, Bible reading, etc. Although The Grief Recovery Method® is **not** a spiritual discipline, it is not against anything in the Bible. In fact, the

truths are in keeping with Biblical truths and the actions are very similar, if not the same, as Biblical actions.

- The Grief Recovery Method® is **not** sanctified (i.e. it is not set apart by God).
- The Grief Recovery Method® is **not** magic. It is not a silver bullet or cure all. In fact, it will get rid of pain and unresolved issues and open you up to feel sadness and reclaim unconflicted memories.
- The Grief Recovery Method® is a tool. Since this tool is not a spiritual discipline, but an educational program, it can be done by anyone.

In addition, since the principles and actions are based on principles of truth that are in keeping with the Bible, they will work, to some degree, with anyone who will do the actions. The same thing is true of 12-Step Programs, which are based upon Bible verses and biblical principles.

Yet, we still need the Holy Spirit, in the use of this tool, to be as effective as possible. Why? **Because of the nature of the heart.**

Jeremiah 17:9-10 (NASB-U), "The heart is more deceitful than all else and is desperately sick; who can understand it? I, the LORD, search the heart, I test the mind, even to give to each man according to his ways, according to the results of his deeds."

Our hearts are more deceitful and sicker than we can even understand. And this deceitfulness and sickness is often hidden in and perpetrated by disappointment with God. Therefore, we need Jehovah God to search our hearts and test our minds, through the power of the Holy Spirit, to offset the deceitfulness of heart!

Before we describe The Grief Recovery Method®, we had better take one moment and talk about grief in general. "What is grief?" *"Grief is the conflicting feelings caused by the end of or change in a familiar pattern of behavior."*[6]

So, "What is The Grief Recovery Method®?" "The Grief Recovery Method® is a combination of the principles and actions of The Grief Recovery Method® that help willing participants discover and complete what was left unresolved or incomplete in their relationships to someone who died, or from whom they are divorced or estranged; and to help them become complete with any other loss events that have affected their lives. The beneficial impact of those actions often open people to emotions they have buried or bypassed because of the accumulation of incomplete losses; and often helps open up spiritual pathways that have been blocked for similar reasons."

Many people whose faith has been damaged by an overwhelming loss, or by an accumulation of losses over a lifetime, have discovered that these actions help to free their spirits and actually enhance their relationship

---

6   John W. James and Russell Friedman, *The Grief Recovery Handbook*, HarperCollins Publishers. Inc., New York, New York, 1998, p. 3.

with God and with their spiritual principles.

The Grief Recovery Method® is the action program for moving beyond loss—one heart at a time!

For those of us who are saved, grief work like The Grief Recovery Method® does not replace faith in Jesus Christ, but includes it. We have enough faith in Jesus Christ to take the necessary steps to face our losses and our pain, rather than deny them. In fact, I have learned that properly navigating The Grief Recovery Method® can and should lead you to Jesus Christ.

The Grief Recovery Method® is a means of facilitating the forgiveness of others. I believe that grief and forgiveness are either synonymous or grief facilitates forgiveness.

This is outstanding information, but we are still left with a very formidable question, "With what we know, why don't we simply do the actions of The Grief Recovery Method® and get well?" Because, information alone does not produce automatically transformation.

That leads to another very formidable question, "Why aren't we taught what to do about grief?" Because, we have received misinformation and myths about grief. That still leads to another question, "Why have we received misinformation and myths about grief?" Because our parents were only able to teach us what they were taught, knew, and had experienced. If they had known better, they would have taught us better, but this is all they had. Therefore, we have been stuck with what was passed on to us and we are passing those things on to our kids and others.

Once again, let's return to what the Bible has to say about these things?

1 Thessalonians 4:13 (NASB-U), "But we do not want you to be uninformed, brethren, about those who are asleep, that you may not **grieve**, as do the rest who have no hope" (*bold type added*).

Paul taught the Thessalonians that they didn't grieve as those who had no hope. There is great Biblical knowledge and there are certain convictions that can make our grieving different from those who don't have such knowledge and convictions. It is not that we do not grieve, but that we do not grieve as do people who have no hope of the resurrection, or eternal life, or anything after this life. Paul is not discussing intellectual Bible concepts or propositions; he is discussing principles that are a part of a person's core belief.

Hope is not a thought, but a principle of a person's core belief. **A person's core belief entails principles for living like hope, trust, love, forgiveness, fear, hatred, prejudice, unforgiveness, etc.** *Principles of one's core belief are much more than intellectual constructs.* These principles inform and impact certain situations in our lives. For those of us who are believers in Jesus Christ, the principle of hope should so inform us and impact us that our grief is different than those who have no hope.

Hope does not reside in the cognitive, or the

emotive, (*i.e. in our thoughts or in our feelings*) but in the intuitive aspects of human personality.[7] *Our intuitions are instinctive or immediate knowledge that is available without the conscious use of reason.* Frank Thomas explained this truth using the core belief of faith, in his outstanding book, *They Like To Never Quit Praisin' God.* Thomas wrote,

> "Faith is born in a 'reasonable encounter,' within
> an emotive context, then moves to reside as a
> principle in the intuitive, informing core belief."[8]

Our intuitive, informing core belief automatically informs us concerning certain important situations in our lives. This core belief is located somewhere in our hearts or human spirits!

In this case, hope automatically informs us and impacts us concerning grief. Therefore, we grieve differently than those who have no hope.

Let me explain more deeply. When you are sinner, it is likely that you have experienced thousands of reasonable encounters, in emotive contexts, where you are let down or disappointed. This disappointment becomes a principle of hopelessness in your core belief. So, when any situation is encountered where hope is required, your core belief automatically informs you and impacts you towards the principle truth that you can depend upon no one and there is no one who can

---

7   Frank A. Thomas, *They Like To Never Quit Praisin' God*, United Church
    Press, Cleveland, Ohio, 1997, p. 9.
8   Frank A. Thomas, *They Like To Never Quit Praisin' God*, United Church
    Press, Cleveland, Ohio, 1997, p. 9.

help you. Therefore, there is little hope of anything better.

On the other hand, if we as believers have been growing in Jesus Christ, we have experienced thousands of reasonable encounters, in emotive contexts, where Jesus comes through for us. These encounters form a principle of hope in our core beliefs. When difficult situations arise, we know without reasoning or thinking about it, that Jesus is going to come and help us out. We have hope that God will straighten things out now, or in the resurrection.

Therefore, we do not grieve as those who have no hope, because hope tempers our grief. We do hurt and struggle through grief, but there is a supernatural element of hope that is mixed with our hurt and struggle!

So grief is an important Biblical concept and we experience that grief differently from those who don't have Jesus Christ.

Nevertheless, sometimes we need a tool like The Grief Recovery Method® to help us do our grief work, do deep repentance, or complete overwhelming losses or an accumulation of loss events. Why? *So that the pain and incompleteness of overwhelming losses or the accumulation of losses do not block our hope, and hence, our intimacy with God!*

chapter five

STERBs and Grief Recovery® Actions

Let me point out that grief is a major Bible subject that is often unseen or overlooked, because of the differences in times and vocabulary.

The translators of the 1995 Update of the NASB translated Hebrew and Greek roots as "grief, grieve, grieved, grieving" 54 times and this does **not** include words like "sorrow," "pain," and others that may, in certain contexts, refer to grief. So, the Bible deals a great deal with grief!

In the last chapter, we began to deal with The Grief Recovery Method®. However, before we move on to the actions of The Grief Recovery Method®, let's return to a major question, "Why do we need to get our hearts back?"

Well, every loss is a grief event—there is

something there that must be grieved! Since we have received misinformation about grief and don't know how to grieve, we wall off pieces of our hearts, so they can't get hurt again. Now think about it! Over our lifetimes, how many losses do we have and how many pieces of our hearts do we have walled off. Right now you are probably thinking, "So what if I've got pieces of my heart walled off ?" Well, let's reconsider a very powerful word from God in Jeremiah 29:13 (NASB-U),

> "You will seek Me and find Me when you search
> for Me with all your heart."

To find God, we must each search for Him with all of our hearts. Unfortunately, we cannot bring all of our hearts to Him, because pieces of them are walled off. Pieces of our hearts have been lost in each unresolved grief event. This causes us to be closed and separated, as opposed to open and connected. And God did not create us to be closed and separated, but open and connected, i.e. intimate—with Him and with one another. *Our hearts are broken, and when our hearts are broken, our heads don't work right and our spirits can't soar.* We engage in Short-Term-Energy-Releasing Behaviors or STERBs.[9]

Yet, there is another impact of not dealing with the things that are walling off pieces of our hearts.

One STERB that is <u>not</u> listed in *The Grief Recovery*

---

9   Russell Friedman and John James, Moving Beyond Loss: Real Answers to Real Questions from Real People, Taylor Trade Publishing, Lanham, Maryland, 2013, pg. 176.

Handbook® is religion. I did not say Christianity or a relationship with God, Jesus Christ, or the Holy Spirit, but religion. Religion is Humanity reaching up to God. Christianity is God reaching down to Humanity. Religion is Humanity working to please God, something that cannot be achieved through work, but only through accepting the price that was paid through Jesus Christ. This pattern of working to please God becomes a short-term energy reducing behavior[10] (STERB) to reduce or hide the pain of loss. Thus many people seek God, not to have a relationship with Him, but to manipulate Him to relieve the pain of their lives. Even though this is very difficult for most of us to see, this STERB can become as addictive and destructive as other STERBs. *Religion drives people, but the love of Jesus Christ draws people.* Since we intellectually know that these things don't work and can be destructive, why and how do we become trapped in them? The answer: When you heart is broken, your head doesn't work right and your spirit can't soar.[11]

The Bible reads in Isaiah 1:5 NLT,

"Why do you continue to invite punishment? Must you rebel forever? **Your head is injured, and your heart is sick"** (bold type added).

---

10 John W. James and Russell Friedman, The Grief Recovery Handbook: The Action Program for Moving Beyond Death, Divorce, and Other Losses, HarperPerennial, New York, New York, 1998, p.78.

11 Russell Friedman and John James, Moving Beyond Loss: Real Answers to Real Questions from Real People, Taylor Trade Publishing, Lanham, Maryland, 2013, pg. 176.

God is asking Israel a rhetorical question about their rebellion. He is trying to get them to see that rebellion only invites punishment. They had to be aware of , the relationship of rebellion to punishment so why did they continue to rebel? The answer is given in the next sentence, "Your head is injured, and your heart is sick!" *i.e. the human spirit is burdened, weighed down, imprisoned, chained, etc. You were created to soar with the eagles, but instead, you're trapped in a barnyard with chickens, with a ball and chain around your leg.*

I can hear some of you saying, "But I ain't in the barnyard of life!" Maybe not, but consider this:

A Tip On "The Race"

Years ago in the Alleghenies a large eagle was shot by a hunter. When he examined the bird, he was amazed to find that one of its claws was held firmly in a strong steel trap from which dangled a 5-foot chain. Although not heavy enough to prevent the creature from flying, the additional weight had wearied the eagle and brought it down within reach of his rifle. So, too, the Christian can be entrapped and brought low spiritually by encumbrances which make him/her incapable of rising to the heights s/he might otherwise attain.

Let me give you two examples of what can happen when our hearts are broken and incapable of releasing energy or feelings in a healthy way.

My example is that of an old fashioned pressure

cooker. A healthy pressure cooker has a rocker and a safety valve to release pressure.

If it were unhealthy, it would have no way of releasing the pressure and this would lead to an explosion.

The Grief Recovery Handbook® uses the example of a steam kettle. A healthy steam kettle releases steam immediately as it builds us, and so should we.

Now, think about a steam kettle heating up, but having a cork in the spout. There can be no relief for the steam kettle. This is dangerous and eventually there is going to be some kind of explosive relief. The same is true of our lives!

All right, we are ready to begin to discuss The Grief Recovery Method®.

These actions should be taken in a group that is run by a Certified Grief Recovery Specialist. You can read about all of this in The Grief Recovery Handbook®, by John James and Russell Friedman.

Action #1: The Lost History Graph

The object of this graph is to make us aware of our losses, so that we can discover what misinformation we were taught directly or absorbed.

Before we move forward, there are some very important principles that I need to touch on here.

First, we should not compare losses! Why? Because, everyone is dealing with pain at 100%. This is very difficult for us to work through in our minds, when we have been used to comparing losses. When one person loses a dog and another a husband, we automatically assume that the person who lost the husband lost more. We do this intellectually, without realizing that the emotional impact of the pain on both persons is 100%. There is no real way of comparing these losses. . The impact of the loss of the dog is 100% to the owner. The impact of the loss of a husband is 100% to the wife, and who is to say that one had a better or more intense relationship than the other. Every relationship is unique. So, they are not to be compared.

Secondly, I want to remind you that you are the only one that can stop your recovery. It is in your hands.

Thirdly, this work is about getting at the emotional truth. The events are not really important. What is important is recognizing and telling the emotional truth. This principle is highlighted by David in Psalm 51:6 (NASB-U),

"Behold, You desire truth in the innermost being, and in the hidden part You will make me know wisdom."

This is also touched on by Jesus in John 8:31-32 (NASB-U),

"So Jesus was saying to those Jews who had believed Him, "If you continue in My word, then you are truly disciples of Mine; and you will know the truth, and the truth will make you free."

What truth is Jesus talking about? The truth of the message of Gospel. What kind of truth was this? This was relational truth, which includes intellectual and especially emotional truth! You shall know the truth (i.e. the intellectual and emotional truth) and the truth shall make you free. So, emotional truth is important to the Bible, the Gospel, and freedom from bondage to sin, Satan, self, and the world.

Remember: The Grief Recovery Method® is no silver bullet or magic potion. It is a tool that can be used to help you recover from loss, complete the incomplete pain of relationships, become aware of emotional truth, etc.

I am aware of the fact that some people will not choose to complete the pain in their relationships. By the way, we believe that all losses and pain happen in the context of relationships. One of the authors of *The Grief Recovery Handbook*®, Russell Friedman, said to me in a personal conversation, "People have a relationship to their pain or addiction status and they get stuck. There comes a point when they, because of their familiarity with their pain, dig in their heals."

The Grief Recovery Method® is a tool that can help you to get unstuck, but the biblical way to recover from an overwhelming loss or an accumulation of losses is to do deep repentance by inviting Jesus into the secret places in your heart.

Steve Chapman wrote a song called "The Secret Place." I want you to listen to the words of this song.

The Secret Place

My heart is like a house,
one day I let the Savior in
There were many rooms,
where we would visit now and then.

But then one day He saw the door,
I knew that day had come too soon
I said, "Jesus, I'm not ready,
for us to visit in that room;
That's a place in my heart,
where even I don't go
I have some things hidden there,
I don't want no one to know."

But He handed me the keys,
with tears of love on His face
He said, "I want to make you clean,
Let Me go in your secret place."

So I opened up the door,
and as the two of us walked in
I was so ashamed,
His light revealed my hidden sin (pain)

But when I think about that room now,
I'm not afraid anymore
Cause I know my hidden sin (pain),
no longer hides behind that door

It was the place in my heart,
where even I wouldn't go
I had some things hidden there,
I didn't want no one to know.
But He handed me the keys,
with tears of love on His face
He made me clean,
I let Him in my secret place.

**The Impediment To Intimacy
(How To Get Our Hearts Back)**

chapter six

More Grief Recovery Method® Actions

Now there are some people who are going to object to going back into the past to deal with anything. They are going to say, "What's in the past should stay in the past and we don't have to drudge up the past to get well?" I have been hearing this since God launched me on this fantastic, relational journey.

My answer to this objection is what God said to me during my preaching of a series of messages entitled "The Ravages of Rejection."

As I was riding in the car on Friday, March 12, 1999, I saw these words stenciled in white on my driver's side rearview mirror: **"Objects in Mirror Are Closer**

than They Appear." The series revolved around the history of the nation of Israel, and Israel's past being closer than it appeared. Forty (40) years appeared to be the distant past, but it was actually closer than it appeared. *Their past was still effecting their present.* Even though rejection had blocked their trust in God forty (40) years earlier, Moses knew that rejection was still impacting Israel in the present.

Believe me, I am all for letting things in the past stay in the past, but unresolved or incomplete loss events and their pain are not in the past, but in the present. It is our goal to do what Paul exhorted in Philippians 3:13 (NASB-U),

> "Brethren, I do not regard myself as having laid hold of it yet; but one thing I do: forgetting what lies behind and reaching forward to what lies ahead."

Paul is talking about living in the present! We are to <u>learn</u> from the past, <u>live</u> in the present, and <u>look</u> towards the future! The question is, "How do we do this?" "How do we forget what lies behind us and reach forward to what lies ahead of us?" How do we live in the present, if we have never been in the present? The only way to move towards this reality is to complete the issues of the past. And how do we do that? Well, let me give you another exhortation by Paul. He said in Romans 6:11 (NASB-U),

"Even so consider yourselves to be dead to sin, but alive to God in Christ Jesus."

Here is one Biblical answer to the question! We need to consider or reckon ourselves to be dead to sin, but alive to God in Christ Jesus. We reckon, consider, or put it down on our accounts that we are dead to sin, but alive to God in Christ Jesus. *This certainly has something to do with deep repentance.* If repentance is deep enough, it will not only take care of present encounters with sin, but past encounters and their residue. Loss issues can be completed by deep repentance, but we essentially have the same question, "How do we do deep repentance?" I have and can explain the biblical process to you, but we still sometimes need a tool to help us facilitate deep repentance. This is where The Grief Recovery Method® comes in.

Let's explore some more of the actions of The Grief Recovery Method®. We have already covered "The Loss History Graph," so we now move to "The Relationship Graph."

Action #2: The Relationship Graph

Remember, we believe that losses and pain occur in the context of relationships. To complete the pain and losses in a relationship, we need to create an accurate picture of the relationship, so that we can deal with the pain and issues that need to be completed.

"The Relationship Graph" is a tool for doing what David talked about in Psalm 51:6 (NASB-U),

> "Behold, You desire truth in the innermost being, and in the hidden part You will make me know wisdom."

God can make us know wisdom through the agency of the revelatory power of the Holy Spirit and the instrumentality of the Word of God. "The Relationship Graph" is a tool that the Holy Spirit can use to help us in the process of discovery!

Remember, these actions should be done under the guidance of a Certified Grief Recovery® specialist.

After "The Relationship Graph" is done, the following actions derive or flow out of that graph.

Action #3: Apologies

The next action is "Making Apologies." I certainly don't need to take a long time talking about these actions, because they are obviously and patently biblical actions and I believe we are now fairly clear on their power to complete pain and loss issues from the past.

Apologies are tools of deep repentance. We are often confused about apologies, because of our misunderstanding of Biblical terminology. In the Bible, people often ask God for forgiveness. This is just another way of saying that they are apologizing or saying they are sorry. Of course, we are talking about godly sorrow.

Because we are modern people, we are much more victims than we are victors. Therefore, we need to be careful of this terminology. When we ask God, or anyone for that matter, for forgiveness, we are trying to control something that is not our responsibility. God is the God of forgiveness and He will automatically extend forgiveness, when we apologize. *So, God will handle forgiveness, but it is our responsibility to apologize.*

This is particularly problematic with people, because we do not control their forgiveness. All that we control is our apologies. Their forgiveness is up to them. I believe Paul touched on this in Romans 12:18 (NASB-U),

"If possible, so far as it depends on you, be at peace with all men."

Action #4: Amends

Peace is **not** always in our hands! We can apologize and people can still choose **not** to forgive us! That is no longer our problem! This does not mean that it will not be sad or unfortunate, but since we cannot control it we need not let it ruin our lives. It is the other person's prerogative to forgive or not forgive.

Additionally, from a biblical perspective, we should also make amends where possible, i.e. we should seek to undo what we have done—when that is possible. Sometimes it is **not** possible! We can't undo murder, adultery, broken trust, etc. We can undo thievery, some lies, and other things.

Let's look at the apology of David to God, with respect to his sin with Bathsheba. David wrote in Psalm 51:1-5 (NASB-U),

"For the choir director. A Psalm of David, when Nathan the prophet came to him, after he had gone in to Bathsheba. Be gracious to me, O God, according to Your lovingkindness; according to the greatness of Your compassion blot out my transgressions. Wash me thoroughly from my iniquity and cleanse me from my sin. For I know my transgressions, and my sin is ever before me. Against You, You only, I have sinned and done what is evil in Your sight, so that You are justified when You speak and blameless when You judge. Behold, I was brought forth in iniquity, And in sin my mother conceived me."

A genuine apology flows from a genuinely repentant heart! This is touched on in Psalm 51:17 (NASB-U),

"The sacrifices of God are a broken spirit; a broken and a contrite heart, O God, You will not despise."

Action #5: Forgiveness

The next Grief Recovery Method® action is "Forgives" or "Forgiveness." Once again, this action is a patently biblical action. Jesus taught in Matthew 6:15 (NASB-U),

> "But if you do not forgive others, then your Father will not forgive your transgressions."

There is much confusion about this verse, but Jesus was **not** teaching that our forgiveness is predicated upon whether we forgive others, because our forgiveness of sins is ultimately based upon the shed blood of Jesus Christ. No, Jesus was teaching that we will **not** be able to experience God's forgiveness, if we are harboring unforgiveness in our hearts.

Writing down things that we need to forgive a person for is an action that helps us to recall and tell the emotional truth about certain events in a relationship.

Down the road, after we have dealt with all of the more tangible relationships that we have, we may also need to forgive God, if we are going to overcome the disappointment that keeps us from being intimate with Him. We are **not** forgiving God because He has done anything wrong, but because we perceive or feel that He has done something wrong in **not** fulfilling our hopes, dreams, and expectations—whether they are Biblical or not.

This is a tricky action, so we do **not** attempt to do a relationship Graph on God, until after we have done all Human relationships on our Loss History Graphs.

Action #6: Significant Emotional Statements

The next Grief Recovery Method® action is to record "Significant Emotional Statements."

This action might **not** seem like it is biblical, but I have already shown you how God made significant emotional statements, when Adam and Eve fell in the Garden of Eden. Significant emotional statements help us to complete communication that is incomplete. We often don't communicate things that we had intended to communicate, because of sin and Human tendencies. This action allows us to become aware of those things that we wished we had said, when the person was alive, married to us, on better terms, etc. This action still involves emotional honesty and telling the emotional truth.

Again, David said in Psalm 51:6 (NASB-U),

"Behold, You desire truth in the innermost being, and in the hidden part You will make me know wisdom."

Notice that this truth is **not** in the mind or intellect, but much deeper than that. *This truth is to be realized in the innermost being, in the Human spirit, in the heart of the heart.*

David doesn't stop there, but goes on to talk about wisdom in the hidden part, i.e. in the immaterial part of

Humanity, in the heart or spirit. *This is emotional and spiritual truth, not just intellectual truth!*

This is about the emotional truth, not the events. We don't have to share every detail of an event with someone else to tell the emotional truth about that event.

Action #7: The Completion Letter

The next action combines the apologies, forgivenesses and significant emotional statements. Next, we compose a "Completion Letter".

This action, along with the others, can be very emotional. It is all right if you display your emotion and it is all right if you don't. Each one of us is unique.

Action #8: Read the Completion Letter

The final action is to read the completion letter to a certified Grief Recovery Specialist® or someone who has been through the program, who understands the principles of sharing, and is safe.

Reading it to another person lines up with the "one another" principle of the New Testament.

> James 5:16 (NASB-U), "Therefore, confess your sins to one another, and pray for one another so that you may be healed. The effective prayer of a righteous man can accomplish much."

In addition, there is something about reading the completion letter out loud to another person that makes all of this work real.

Now here is a huge point: It is important that we say the word "Goodbye" at the end of our letters. This is a tool for completing the pain or other incomplete things in a relationship that is connected to a loss event. When we say, "Goodbye," we are not saying goodbye to the relationship, but to the pain and incompleteness of the relationship!

The actions of The Grief Recovery Method® are very similar to biblical actions.

All of these actions are tools for doing what Paul stated in Philippians 3:13-14 (NASB-U),

> "Brethren, I do not regard myself as having laid hold of it yet; but one thing I do: forgetting what lies behind and reaching forward to what lies ahead, I press on toward the goal for the prize of the upward call of God in Christ Jesus."

These are tools. If you don't want to use these tools, you don't have to. Use whatever tools you believe will work for you, but on the basis of my 41 years of pastoral ministry and advising people, and the 12 years of using The Grief Recovery Method®, I would recommend these tools. They are **not** spiritual disciplines; they are **not** sanctified; but they are in keeping with the Bible and they are effective.

**The Impediment To Intimacy
(How To Get Our Hearts Back)**

chapter seven

Completion, Emotional Health and Spiritual Maturity

As we end this book, we come to the idea of completion. This is commonly referred to as "closure." We cannot complete a relationship, because relationships are eternal. However, we can complete our attachment to negative emotions.

Is completion a biblical idea? Well, the Bible says in Colossians 1:28 (NASB-U),

"We proclaim Him, admonishing every man and

teaching every man with all wisdom, so that we may present every man complete in Christ."

The word "complete" is the Greek word *teleios*. This word has caused a lot of misunderstanding and misteaching, because of its unfortunate translation in the KJV, where it is translated "perfect." The meaning of the word is "having reached its end, i.e. complete" (*NASB Greek & Hebrew Dictionary [Updated Edition]*). So, the word can mean that someone or something is perfect as having reached its end or being completed. When used of people, a better translation is probably "mature," and it is so translated in a number of verses of the 1995 Update of the NASB.

Hence, in this verse, Paul wanted to present the Colossians believers as complete, having reached their designed end, or mature in Christ. I like this and it is very much related to completing the pain in our loss events, so that we might reach the end that God intended for us. Is that end maturity in Christ? I believe it is!

Paul not only talked about presenting every believer as complete in Christ, but he gave some of his ways of doing this, which included preaching Christ, admonishing or confronting every believer, and teaching every believer with all wisdom. Paul's goal and a major Grief Recovery Method® goal are very much compatible, i.e. presenting us as complete or mature in Christ as compared to helping people complete the pain in their relationships so that they might be mature.

Now please keep in mind that if we had handled

and continued to handle sins (loss events) with immediate apologies, forgiveness, and significant emotional statements, there would be no need for "Loss History Graphs," "Relationship Graphs," and "Completion Letters," except to clean up those things that we missed. *In Christian language, this is called "keeping short accounts with God."*

But, because of sin and human tendencies, we are never complete in our apologies, forgiveness, and significant emotional statements. When we accumulate a sufficient number of unresolved or incomplete loss events, our hearts will be hardened to the point that we cannot come fully present with anyone—including God. This is where the relationship graph, apologies, forgiveness, significant emotional statements, and completion letters come in. They allow us to resolve or complete the pain of things that we did not handle in the moment.

Are you beginning to understand what it is that we are completing?

You cannot forget your loved one. Your relationship with your loved one is not over. The physical relationship may be over, but the emotional and psychological relationship continues on. *What will be completed is the pain that has marred your memories of your loved one.*

All right! As we come to the end of this book, we have been talking about how to get our hearts back. So, for one last time, "How do we get our hearts back?"

We get our hearts back by completing the pain in past

relationships. So, I am sorry to tell you that successfully completing The Grief Recovery Method® will not end your sadness; it will complete your pain. Please get this! Successfully completing The Grief Recovery Method® will complete what is incomplete so that the pain of the event is resolved, but sadness is a perfectly normal residue. In fact, The Grief Recovery Method® allows one to get the normal feelings of sadness back and the good memories that were conflicted with pain. The Grief Recovery Method® can be likened to physical healing. If you have ever hurt or cut yourself physically, there can be a lingering effect if the injury is severe. After it is healed, bumping or pressing against that spot can still produce pain. The pain reminds you of what happened, even though it is healed. In fact, if there were no pain in that spot it would not be a good sign.

That's why holidays can be painful. Holidays often bump the loss event and we feel some of the soreness of being reminded of the loss.

Successfully completing The Grief Recovery Method® will not only open our hearts to new relationships, it will allow us to be current or fully present in all of our relationships. When we sin or have incomplete loss events, they interrupt our fellowship with God, other people, and even ourselves. If we handle these sins or loss events through apologies, repentance, forgiveness, and significant emotional statements to God and all other appropriate people, we will stay current or fully present in those relationships. God is a God of the here and now! He is the great "I

AM!"

The sons of Korah wrote this song in Psalm 46:1 (NASB-U),

> "For the choir director. A Psalm of the sons of Korah, set to Alamoth. A Song. God is our refuge and strength, **a very present help** in trouble" (*bold type added*).

God is a very present help in the time of need. So, we need to become fully present to experience his help in all of our times of need.

Now, what does it mean to be authentically present? Authentic presence requires a high level of energy, openness, and focus. When we are drowsy or lethargic, closed or skeptical, and scattered or lack concentration, it is very difficult to be fully present.

When we come to church, we want to have energy, we want to be open to the movement of the Holy Spirit, and we want to be focused on what is going on.

The authors of *Executive E.Q.*, which is about emotional intelligence, have developed a wonderful formula to explain what they call "authentic presence."

$$(A \times C) - (U \times E) = AP$$
$$(\text{Attentiveness} \times \text{Concern}) - (\text{Ulterior Motive} \times \text{Entitlement}) = \text{Authentic Presence}[12]$$

---

12 Robert K. Cooper and Ayman Sawaf, *Executive EQ, A Pedigree Book* Published by The Berkley Publishing Group, New York, New York, 1997, p. 69.

Attentiveness multiplied by concern for the other person is the positive side of "Authentic Presence." To have "authentic presence" we must be attentive to people and the situations that are around us.

In addition, we must have genuine concern for people. When attentiveness is multiplied by concern, we have a positive measure of "authentic presence."

But, there are also some things that can detract from "authentic presence." They are ulterior motive and entitlement. When we have ulterior motives, this detracts from our "authentic presence." An ulterior motive is an underlying selfish or dishonorable motive.

When we have an attitude of entitlement, this also detracts from "authentic presence." Americans have a noticeable attitude of entitlement.

When ulterior motive is multiplied by entitlement, we have a measure of these things that detract from "authentic presence."

Now, when we subtract the negative measure from the positive measure, we are left with some measure of "authentic presence." Each element of the equation is rated on a scale of one to ten. The rating of "authentic presence" can be anywhere from −100 to 100.

The Grief Recovery Method® can help in the pursuit of "Authentic presence."

When we get our hearts back, we will not only be complete, mature, open to new relationships, and fully present in our relationships, we will be healthy. Doing Grief Recovery Method® work or completing the pain of past losses allows us to be healthy in our love of others and ourselves.

We need to love others and ourselves in a healthy manner.

One of the impacts of unhealthy self-love is self-rejection and one of the symptoms of self-rejection is that negatives adhere to us, while positives   and affirmations bounce off of us.

When we have done deep repentance, whether solely through the work of the Holy Spirit or with the aid of the tool of The Grief Recovery Method®, we will be more equipped to live out what Jesus taught in Mark 12:29-31 (NASB-U),

> Jesus answered, "The foremost is, 'HEAR, O ISRAEL! THE LORD OUR GOD IS ONE LORD; AND YOU SHALL LOVE THE LORD YOUR GOD WITH ALL YOUR HEART, AND WITH ALL YOUR SOUL, AND WITH ALL   YOUR   MIND, AND WITH   ALL   YOU STRENGTH.'

The second is this, 'You shall love your neighbor as yourself.' There is no other commandment greater than these."

Notice that we are to love God with all of our hearts, i.e. all of our emotions; with all of our souls, i.e. all of our personalities; with all of our minds, i.e. all of our thoughts; and with all of our strength, i.e. with all of our bodies. This cannot be lived out, unless we have gotten our hearts back!

The second commandment is similar to the first commandment, we are to love our neighbors as ourselves. This certainly intimates a healthy love of ourselves and of others!

Therefore, this verse requires that we do deep repentance, with or without The Grief Recovery Method®, so that we can remove the impediment of disappointment with God and get our hearts back! When we get our hearts back, we will be able to find God and enter into deep, passionate, delicious intimacy with Him. As I end this book, I return to a previous realization.

On Monday afternoon, November 18th, 2002, I had another epiphany. They seem to come more rapidly and more powerfully, perhaps because of the grief work that I have done...perhaps because I am fifty...perhaps because all the reading I have done...perhaps because of the years of struggling and surrendering my life to God, through ministry...perhaps?

As I was coming to the end of *The Journey of Desire*, by John Eldredge, I came across this paragraph, "I believe we must add two spiritual disciplines to everyday life. The first is worship. We must adore God deliberately, regularly. The other is grief. We must allow a time of sorrow to do our own personal sowing. I see no other way to care for our hearts."[13]

After reading this, the following truth broke upon me like the newborn sun breaking over the horizon and into my room on an expectant spring morning: The Grief

---

13   John Eldredge, *The Journey Of Desire*, Thomas Nelson Publishers, Nashville, Tennessee, 2000, p. 189.

Recovery® Program is but a tool, a very excellent tool, but alas…still a tool. But **grief itself** is a spiritual discipline that is put forth and described all through the Bible; experienced by Jesus Christ to procure our salvation and as our example **(a man of sorrows and acquainted with grief)**; and arranged by the Father to cleanse and heal our hearts and woo us back to Himself **(but the LORD was pleased to crush Him, putting Him to grief)**, where He will one day wipe away every loss, pain, sorrow, sadness, and grief in heaven.

Until then, we must allow time for suffering, sorrow, and grief to do their perfect work. Is that what the psalmist has realized in Psalm 126:4-6 (NLT),

"Restore our fortunes, LORD, as streams renew the desert. Those who plant in tears will harvest with shouts of joy. They weep as they go to plant their seed, but they sing as they return with the harvest."

Sorrow is our sowing and rejoicing is our reaping! As we continue to make time for personal times of sowing, we shall reap more and more joy.

- It is working through grief that will prepare our hearts for true, living, intimate worship of Jehovah God.
- It is working through grief that will allow us to be fully present enough to give all that we are in worship to God, because of all that He is.

- It is working through grief that will allow us to enter into passionate, unabashed, delicious, breathtaking intimacy with the Lover of our Souls, i.e. Jesus Christ!

As praise is a means of taking territory back from the devil and worship is the means of ratifying the covenant promises of God, so working through grief is the means of recapturing and living through our hearts, so that praise and worship might be might be released unto their full potential.

We are most alive when we are genuinely worshipping God, and healthy grieving keeps the lifeblood of worship flowing. This begs for a living heart that is emotionally healthy!

32602299R10056

Made in the USA
Middletown, DE
11 June 2016